Spilled Coffee, Marriage, & White Sheets

Jesus Guided
Self-Reflection

BY
KATIE PIRTLE

Whole Life
PRESS
a division of SpeakTruth Media Group LLC

Spilled Coffee, Marriage, & White Sheets
Jesus Guided Self-Reflection
Copyright © 2023, Katie Pirtle

Publisher: WholeLife Press a division of
SpeakTruth Media Group, LLC
PO Box 1448, Crockett TX 75835-7448

Book design by SpeakTruth Media Group, LLC.

ISBN: 979-8-9857296-9-6 *(pb)*

Books are available in quantity for promotional or premium use. For information on discounts and terms, please inquire at order   speaktruthmedia.com.

Printed in the USA

DEDICATION

To my loving husband

and

the Ranch Wives' Bible Study Group.

CONTENTS

Introduction: Let's Go to the Cleaners, *page 7*

Chapter 1: A Good Cup of Coffee, *page 13*

Chapter 2: Coffee Stains, *page 22*

Chapter 3: Favorite Sheets, *page 30*

Chapter 4: Wash Cycles & Stain Removal, *page 45*

Chapter 5: Love, *page 61*

Chapter 6: Time Well Spent, *page 93*

Chapter 7: All-in-All, *page 99*

Let's Go to the Cleaners

I was sitting on my porch in deep thought, sorting through all the negatives satan was laying before me regarding our first evening Bible study when I caught a glimpse of my son's chair sitting in our open yard. This chair was nothing big or fancy; it was small and straightforward, randomly placed in our yard by our youngest, who liked to watch the cars go by in the street. But God made it extraordinary to me.

God let this little chair reveal stillness in a busy world, providing a moment of reflection in myself and bringing me peace instead of chaos. I was so caught up in what I wanted our Bible study to look like that I'd been downing myself for not making the first night something spectacular. I forgot who was in charge.

God's slight nudge with the chair pulled me back where I needed to be. I needed to be still because this was His Bible study, not mine. I needed to reflect on myself and how to serve Him better while He worked in our group. I needed to remain in His peace and not the enemy's chaos. So, I prayed about why I felt the way I did and handed it over to the Lord. I asked Him to give me something extraordinary to share for our following Bible study and, oh friends, how He came through. A few minutes later, my friend sent me a video entitled, *What's Hurting Your Relationship* by Steven Furtick, which was phenomenal.

If you have not watched it, you should!

During my morning shenanigans, I like to have my coffee in bed. I am extremely cautious. When doing so because my sheets are white. One set is my favorite; nothing compares to their softness and luxury. I am a texture person, and you have no clue how crazy I am about these sheets. I'm pretty sure the saints themselves have blessed the perfection of their fibers; that's how wonderful they are. I am pretty sure they were made in heaven just for me. In my opinion, they are perfect.

So, I am in bed with my phone and coffee, ready to watch this video. One minute into the program, I kid you not, my coffee cup falls out of my hand! How could this happen? I immediately went into panic mode. I lost my mind a few times, and it was chaos. Aggravation arose in the middle of this mess, and I immediately stopped. As loud as I could in my head, I shouted, "Not today, satan!" I acknowledged his plan to throw me off course and stopped him from what he was about to do. I picked up the towel at the end of the bed and put it where I was sitting to soak up the wetness. I changed my shirt, grabbed what was left of that goodness in a cup, and watched that video. God is good, let me tell you, and through that video, He revealed what I needed to hear and what needed to be shared with my Bible study group.

I asked myself, why did I get so aggravated? It's just coffee and sheets! It's not the end of the world. As a result, several things began running through my head:

#1 – That was a good cup of coffee

#2 – Coffee stains everything it touches

#3 – Those were my favorite sheets

#4 – Now, I face the process of washing them.

Not that washing sheets is a big deal, but it is time-consuming in my busy day. I had created a mess for myself, and satan was trying to distract me while God was waiting patiently for me to get it together.

I knew in the back of my thoughts that if I did not take care of that coffee spill ASAP, it would create a stain that would be harder for me to remove later. I began thinking about that stain and how the effect of its residue would worsen over time. My thoughts began to wander, and I realized this scene had a more significant application. Subsequently,

11

this question arose: why is it when something is

spilled onto our marriage with the potential to stain

it that, the offender is not stripped down right then

and quickly put through the wash process? With

that question in mind, let's go to the cleaners

together.

CHAPTER 1

A Good Blend of Coffee

Coffee is not good all the time. Sometimes it doesn't have the perfect helping of sugar, or it's too strong or too weak, or perhaps you're out of your favorite creamer. You expect it to be good because you take your time to make it just how you like it. But when ingredients are missing, and you must improvise, that changes your cup of goodness.

THE MANY BLENDS

There are *different blends* of coffee, just like there are different blends in marriage. The most decadent blend of marriage we can have is the one that is brewed in God's Word and has Him as the head of everything we do. Coffee isn't good all the time, just like marriage isn't. There are different brews in the stages of marriage.

THE BREAKFAST BLEND

Early on, there is *the Breakfast Blend.* Here couples learn about the real world and what being an adult is all about. You have found the one you love and want to create a life with and have entered the newly wedded circle. Everything is mild and smooth. Blinded by all the excitement of your future dreams, you're dwelling on the newness of

14

marriage. It also means getting a real job, taking on responsibilities for yourself, and learning how to make ends meet.

Typically in the early years of marriage, couples think they have it all together. Life is grand and flowing as you walk through getting the keys to your first home and possibly celebrating the new life of a child or two and just living in a dream.

THE CLASSIC BLEND

The Classic Blend comes as the marriage continues and you realize that all the newness has worn off and reality has set in. The dark roast of when that cute thing they used to do has become the biggest pain in your rear. Here you find out love isn't just a feeling; it's an action, and you must do it

15

even though you don't feel like it. In this stage, you may even question if marriage was the right choice.

Traveling down this portion of the marriage road may bring you to a place where God is being called upon the most since He's the only thing keeping you from strangling your spouse! Yes, I said it, but you know you have thought about it. We are all human.

This may be a time of growing apart and then trying to rekindle what you once had. We pursue relighting that flame that once flickered brightly. Here we realize that looks fade and size 2 isn't forever, and for goodness sake, who thought coming up with the supper menu *every* week would be this stinkin' hard? We get tired, unmotivated, and lazy, and what was once something we enjoyed making, careful that it stayed hot and had the perfect helpings of our favorite flavorings, is now a watered-down iced coffee on the go.

Just like coffee, marriage can get watered down and flavorless when the perfect blend of time, love, and Jesus is not present. Here we must figure out that if Jesus isn't driving our thoughts and actions, our marriage will eventually grow cold and become tasteless and fail. The love that God has for us never fails; He pours it out over us even when we don't deserve it. His love for us is the perfect example of how we should love our spouses. Yeah, I know that is a hard pill to swallow. I choked too. But we must drink that pill down.

Give yourself some grace, and give grace to your spouse too. Life is hard. We are all growing through life and hopefully changing and adapting to become whom God has designed us to be. Build up your home and marriage by encouraging one another and loving fearlessly. This stage of marriage is crucial. Taking time to build the foundation of your marriage will keep it afloat when torrents of trouble rush in. This is where you find the true meaning of love.

THE BLACK SILK BLEND

Black Silk is the "been-through-it-all" stage. Here you see the years piling up. Years of sticking it out, trusting in God, and still holding on to the one that has weathered all the storms with you. This stage of marriage is when you are grateful you have someone who loves you for who you are, no matter what you look like. It's God's brew of marriage, so strongly brewed in Jesus that the devil doesn't even dare try and stir it up.

Your foundation is so strong together in the Lord that you're no longer bothered when trouble comes. Your wisdom, knowledge, and awe-struck wonder of the Lord, and His Word, shields and protects you. This is the unshakeable stage we all long to make it to in our marriage. Here you are so deeply rooted in love that you know you have finally made it to the "I-don't-know-how-we-did-it" stage.

The devil has tried to use every tactic possible to stain you and your marriage. Our mess-ups and setbacks may challenge us but never forget that failures don't define who we are. They make us stronger in our walk with the Lord.

We can also consider marriage as a brewing process.

THE BREWING PROCESS

#1 – Water, Filter, and Coffee Stage

Where we dream of the goodness of what is to come, saturating and filtering all those lovely grounds with the heat of new love and reveling in the mixture of two becoming one.

#2 – Steeping Stage

We realize love is a lot more than an emotion, and when things get heated, we learn to lean on Jesus as He filters through our relationship touching every ground so that He can form the richest blend of unity.

#3– Touching the Soul with Goodness Stage

Here we praise the Lord for His faithfulness and guidance toward an unbreakable marriage because we built that foundation in Him.

Reflection time...

What blend of coffee are you experiencing right

now in your marriage?

_____

_____

_____

_____

Is your cup of coffee still good? _____

If not, what is it lacking? _____

_____

_____

_____

What could make it better? _____

_____

_____

_____

CHAPTER 2

Coffee Stains

As soon as the coffee hit those sheets the ugly brown stain had already started to take hold in the fibers of my precious sheets. Satan knew what he was doing when I spilled that coffee. He had been waiting there the whole time because he wanted to distract me. That's what satan does. He is the stain of all stains therefore we must recognize him and his sneaky plans. With this little spill he tried to take something small and magnify it. He wants to blow things out of proportion to distract us so that we miss what God is trying to bless us with.

Let me tell you something. When you are on fire for the Lord you become a bigger threat to the enemy than before and he can't stand that. He wants to get you where you're weakest and manipulate all the emotions he can. Satan knew if he got me aggravated, I wouldn't receive what the Lord was going to give me. By calling him by name and letting him know victory was not his for the taking, I stopped him cold in his tracks.

God has given us power over this stain-making enemy. Luke 10:19 says: *Behold, I have given you authority to tread on serpents and scorpions, and over all the power of the enemy, and*

23

nothing shall hurt you. That's right, go ahead, brush those shoulders off, do a little dance, and thank the Big Guy upstairs because He has empowered us beyond what we can comprehend.

Satan might have thought he stained me with aggravation at first, but being rooted in God's Word has given me the ability to see his handy work. I may have briefly covered that spilled coffee with a towel, but I didn't let it take root in those sheets. I didn't let the aggravation of the mess I had made stop me from obeying God. The towel, I would like to explain, is symbolic of a time out so that I could stop the stain maker in his tracks. It bought time to think about what was happening then, then process how I would handle the situation. In that pause, I could listen to the patient One above whispering to me, warning me not to let the enemy sabotage this moment.

You see, we get so caught up in our emotions that we let them ruin the moments given to us to grow. The Bible tells us we are to be controlled by the Holy Spirit, not by our emotions. Like our bodies and minds, our sinful nature taints our feelings. That's because they need control. Placing that towel was a positive move in my situation as it allowed me to recognize fully what was happening and helped me gain control of my emotions and submit them to the Lord.

Taking that pause, I grew spiritually in my relationship by leaning on the Lord. I could control my thoughts and emotions and do what I was instructed. We can use the same method in our marriages. James 1:19-20 says, *Know this, my beloved brothers: let every person be quick to hear, slow to speak, slow to anger, for man's anger does not produce the righteousness of God.* Let me briefly expound on this verse about how to apply it when dealing with our spouses and not stained sheets.

BE QUICK TO HEAR!

Being quick doesn't mean hearing what you want to hear and jumping to conclusions. It simply means to slow down and listen to what the person is saying. Hear the emotion driving the conversation. Step back from your self-centeredness, quit taking offense, and listen to the words. Listen to the speaker's heart, which is the first step to being others-centered. Take time to understand where the emotion stems from. It may be from hurt feelings,

26

anger, or misunderstanding. Whatever it is, see past the negative to hear and understand why the words are being said.

BE SLOW TO SPEAK!

Much of our anger results from selfishness. Perhaps it's wanting to have the last word or just wanting to be heard. Or maybe we need to be right or have the good ol' one-upper comments. *Slow to speak* means first thinking about the words flowing from our mouths. Ask yourself, "*Does this reflect Jesus? Are my words spoken out of love, or am I going to have to apologize after I say it?*" *Slow to speak* means filtering your words through an understanding that you are speaking life or death into a person, which is a good way to practice being others-centered.

BE SLOW TO ANGER!

We must understand that our anger (wrath) does not accomplish the righteousness of God. Anger almost always defends or promotes our own agenda. James distinguishes between "human anger" (or the anger of man) and God's anger. Everything God feels and expresses is righteous, including His anger. Unbridled human anger, by contrast, is nearly always an expression of selfishness, fear, or the desire to be in control of the world around them. Friends, we must be rooted in God, His Word, and His divine plan for our lives. He needs to be the center of our thoughts and actions.

Reflection time...

What are some things (big or small) satan has tried to magnify in your marriage?

_____

_____

_____

_____

What emotions stem from these things?

_____

_____

_____

_____

What are some ways you can "put a towel on it" to gain control of your emotions?

_____

_____

_____

CHAPTER 3

Favorite Sheets

Just like my precious sheets, your marriage should

be your favorite and you should want to do

everything you can to protect it. So why do we

allow what has spilled on it to stain it? We let things

that have hurt our feelings or angered us fester. We

put them in our little "I will remember that later"

box for ammo. Eventually that will turn into resentment, unforgiveness, irritation and hate.

Communication and forgiveness are key. It pays to remember that we are washed in the blood of Jesus and no sin will stain us when we ask for forgiveness with a sincere heart. When our hearts are heavy with conviction we are to submit in prayer and bring our sins to Jesus for them to be washed clean. There is no difference in marriage. We all mess up. We say things we don't mean. We are human.

We are called to love like Jesus loved. Those are some big shoes to fill in this fallen world we reside in. He is the perfect example of forgiving those who did him wrong. Starting in John 13, Jesus sets the perfect example of His love. He washes His disciples' feet just hours before the crucifixion. He places Himself in the lowest spot in the house and puts His words into action. He could have easily asked one of the servants to do this activity to show His disciples what He was instructing them to do. But instead, He showed them Himself. He acted with humility and washed each of their feet.

In Luke 22:23 it says the disciples entered the room debating who was the greatest among themselves. Yet none of them possessed the true acts of leadership as Jesus did. Each of the disciples would have washed Jesus's feet, but they wouldn't have washed each other's. They weren't girded with humility, but rather they were strapped with pride to prove who was better.

I can only imagine the thoughts of His disciples as Jesus washed their feet. The Son of God, on the ground, washing the feet of people who were about to betray him. What an amazing act of love and example of leadership! In the last hours of His life, Jesus was serving and instructing His disciples on loving one another, not placing themselves higher than each other.

People just like you and me crucified Him on a wooden cross, cursed Him, spit on Him, beat, battered, and bruised Him, yet He lived a life knowing He would die for the people who were going to do this. Although the crucifixion was influenced by the devil himself, had they fully believed in God and had a relationship with Him, perhaps they could have seen the plan of satan.

Instead, Jesus died on that cross and showed us the ultimate example of love. He doesn't hate us for any of this, and He didn't harbor it in His little bag of "I'm going to get you back for that." He simply led by example. Do unto others as you want to others to do to you.

We must forgive as Jesus does. Yes, I'm sure there is some eye-rolling going on at this point, and the thoughts of "I'm not touching anyone's dirty feet" is pressing in your mind. But if Jesus, the Son of God, can get on the ground and scrub the feet of His friends who are about to betray Him, you can gird yourself in humility and lead by example just as He did. You can forgive your spouse who has wronged you and not set yourself higher. You, too can instruct by example how to love like Jesus by your actions in not repaying evil for evil.

Remember, we aren't fighting against each other. We are fighting against the enemy's influence in our lives. We are all created equal in the Lord's eyes. None of us are better than the rest. No one understands your pain like Jesus does. But He has given us the instructions for forgiveness, and we are to obey Him. We live in a world captivated by the dark forces and everything in his corner. Marriages aren't taken seriously anymore. Maybe it's comparing what you have to everyone else, thinking the grass is greener on the other side. We steadily create stain after stain don't even realize it because that's the new normal.

Focusing on things in this world removes our focus from Jesus and puts the spotlight on the enemy. Satan will distract you with whatever he can. Money, fame, lust, what your best friend has, pretty much everything on the other side of the fence that is forbidden.

Geez, didn't anyone learn from Adam and Eve? They had the entire garden and were told not to eat from one tree, but because of oh-so-sneaky-snake satan, they made the one choice that altered their lives forever. And here we are, still toying with his lie-filled fruits. And we are letting the seeds from that wrong fruit sprout in us and take root.

When we are in unity with one another, our choices affect those we are bonded with. Your actions reflect your thoughts, and your thoughts reflect what's in your heart. I need to ask you, what is your heart reflecting? Are you reflecting Jesus and His instruction to love and forgive? Are you leading by Jesus' example in the hours of betrayal or hurt, not repaying evil for evil? Are the things you're holding on to worth it? Are those words spoken out of anger still haunting you? Or perhaps you are still holding on to hurt feelings of the forgotten birthday or anniversary. Letting these things take root in your life is the stain of the enemy and your poor decisions.

Communicate with your spouse when things get heated, or your feelings get hurt. Stop taking offense whenever something rubs you wrong or doesn't align with your preferences. Bring these issues to the table and work through them. Ask God for insight and understanding in your marriage. Ask for a new perspective when communicating with one another. With God as the head of your marriage, you cannot fail.

Your marriage is supposed to be like those favorite sheets, something you enjoy and feel safe in. Marriage is a unity with the one who makes you feel encouraged, empowered, respected and loved. It shouldn't be made into a war zone. Please don't allow the enemy to pour things into it to make you want to discard them or change our view or feelings on what is most important to us. Satan's plan is nothing new. He steals. He kills and destroys. Recognize these things in your marriage, even the small things, and don't allow yourself to fall into his trap. It may require a very hard apology, a loud gulp of swallowing pride, a hug even though you don't want to, and a forgiving heart, but these steps are necessary for a successful marriage.

My husband is my absolute favorite. However, we have had our share of hurt feelings and unkind words spoken. But having God as the head of my heart has allowed me to push through those less than enjoyable times. For that I am grateful. This is a No Stain Zone, and the enemy isn't welcome here. The word divorce holds no ground in my home nor should it in yours. These next four words are very important as they are steps to the no stain process.

STOP

Acknowledge what and who is causing the emotion. Filter through your thoughts in silence before you speak. Train yourself to not let your emotions run your actions. Stop your emotions in their tracks before you speak death over your spouse.

PRAY

Bring your negative thoughts and emotions before God in prayer. Ask Him for the truth and to show you where the poison of satan is dwelling and staining. Pray that when you speak you have truth and honorable meaning in your words. We quickly want to be heard, to be right, or to have the last word that we discard our spouse's feelings. We must humble ourselves before the Lord to the point that we die to our self-centeredness. It doesn't matter if anyone knows your side of the story or you get the last word in. What matters is that you glorify God in your actions and words. We are so saturated with me, me, me, and I'm right, and you're wrong, that there is no room for God's grace to shine through. Pray that God helps you stop such a poisonous spiral in your thoughts so you can have more others-centered actions.

FORGIVE

Quit harping on the mistake that was made. Let it go, friend. Your spouse can't move past it,

and neither can you if you keep throwing old issues
on the table. Jesus didn't go through everything He
did to have you to hold on to all the wrong that has
ever been done to you. Forgive or excuse or pardon
or whatever word you need to use, just don't harbor
it. Truly let it go. I'm so thankful we have a
forgiving God, and that He doesn't hold our wrongs
over our heads. Keeping track of wrongs is
exhausting. Let offenses go so growth can happen
in your spiritual relationship with God. Forgiveness
is growth.

EXAMPLE

A fine example of humility and forgiveness
has been given for us to follow. Jesus left His
royalties in heaven and humbled Himself to the
point of a bondservant to live among us. He showed

41

us how to live a life that glorified God. His friends betrayed Him, sent Him to His death yet He forgave them. We have no excuse. The example has been set. Follow it.

We all love the new sparkly thing until the shine wears off or it starts causing us problems. A major problem with marriage today is that so few people seem willing to work through the tough times. When marriage is not fun anymore we discard it and start over again. That is a vicious cycle of false love.

Reflection time...

What is your favorite thing about your marriage?

_____

_____

What makes you want to fight for it?

_____

_____

_____

Are you harboring anything that needs to be

forgiven? _____ Why are you harboring it?

_____

_____

_____

Do you have good communication or has silent

treatment taken over?

_____

_____

Where have you allowed the enemy to take root?

_____

_____

And what is your plan of action? Revive or neglect?

_____

_____

_____

CHAPTER 4

Wash Cycle and Stain Removal

Just as we strip a bed of its linens we need to strip ourselves down and humbly come before the Lord. I'm sensing an eyeroll here. I know, I thought I was perfect too. It's ok. We can be surprised together. To come before God and for Him to cleanse us we must be transparent. It's not like he doesn't already know everything about us. I mean He *is* the one who created us. He has provided the ultimate stain remover, but we must be willing to go through the necessary steps to receive it.

I'm going to get real with you on a personal level here. This is one of the hardest things to admit but I was the biggest problem in my marriage. I don't like to be wrong. I'm stubborn. And I can't stand not being in control. There I said it. That looks even worse on paper then it did in my head. But it's the truth. I focused so much on what aggravated me about my husband and what I thought he needed to change that I didn't see that it was me.

Was he a complete angel? Well, no, but that isn't for me to worry about. Through lots of prayer and tears and nothing changing, God revealed to me what I needed to focus on. And that focus was the change that needed to happen in me. You wanna talk about being mad? I had an all-out temper tantrum with the Lord. I was like, "You must be kidding me! Didn't You hear what he said? Don't You see the things he's doing? What about me and how I feel?"

I had to become transparent with God. It was far from easy. Everything I laid down about my husband, God laid down something about me. It hurt; I'm not going to lie. This is where the painful journey of dying to my own selfishness began. Slowly the transformation in myself brought change. God took me to the cleaners and stripped me bare.

God calls us women to build up our homes. Often, it's us that must do all the changing and rearranging before our husbands do. We, as wives, set the tone for our home, and mine was set for destruction. God revealed to me that there were several things we would be held accountable for. Our relationship with Him, our marriage, our children, and how we treat others. That's right, all that! And I'm over here tearing mine down and didn't even know it.

I did all the things I thought the Bible said to do. I tended to my home, made sure it was neat and tidy, took care of the yard, and the kids, made sure I had food on the table and was at church every time the door was open. In my eyes, you couldn't get any better than that.

But that's where I was messing up, I was looking with *my* eyes and not God's. I was doing all these things but with bitterness in my heart. I wasn't

48

receiving anything in return, and I was overwhelmed with self-pity. I felt weighed down because I was always the one that had to sacrifice. I felt that all I did went unseen, and I wasn't appreciated. I used those complaints as my driving force. I demanded change, and it wasn't going to be in me. I was letting satan set my husband and me up for failure. Nagging Nancy was in full swing. Comeback Karen was my middle name, and Point Making Peggy insisted on being heard.

God sees things *differently* than we do, in case you don't know it by now.

No one's process is the same, just like everyone's sheets are not the same color or brand. We are all different. But what causes the stains on our sheets or on our marriages are all the same. Irritation, unforgiveness, feeling unappreciated,

49

carrying resentment, and being offended isn't new to the game, especially in my house. I let these things fester, and I had several bags of "Oh, that's going to burn when I use that later." I had negative ammo stacked up to the ceiling. I had comebacks for days, and good ones, too. I couldn't wait for him to slip up. I was waiting for the perfect opportunity to hurt him like he hurt me. I would fight that fire with fire and then feel like the victim after it was over.

You see, I was influenced by the enemy, and the Lord helped me see it. He shined His light on me and gave me a new perspective on this mess I was creating. Friends, I was tearing my man apart! Everything he did, I nitpicked apart. Every time he moved, I had something to say. I had already set him up for failure before he had a chance to do right.

You know, to this day, my husband has never once gotten upset about me spending money on myself or questioned why I do things the way I do. He just goes with the flow, and whatever makes me happy is good with him. God has blessed me with a wonderful man. He never holds things against me, and as quickly as an argument starts, he's normally over it. I was one of those; it took a day or two to get over it fully. But I have learned that during that time, God was showing me how to work on those things that I could potentially harbor in my heart. I'm no longer a "*stay angry for days*" wife. God is processing my emotions and showing me how to correct where I have messed up and accept when I am wrong.

In the times when things get really heated, we have made a deal to both back up and take time to cool off before we discuss the issue. We throw the towel on it until we can handle it properly. This has been the best strategy for us as a couple. We must realize as women we are not the only ones with emotions. Our men get their feelings hurt too.

As a matter a fact, that was one of the things God revealed to me. The reasons my husband would lash out at me was because I had done something that really hurt his feelings. I never realized it because I was too caught up in me, myself, and I. Yes, all three. I was the victim in my own destruction. I was self-centered and not God-centered.

Satan is no dummy. He knows where you

struggle as a couple, and he will rock that ship just to watch you fall overboard and tread water. He's going to try and stain your marriage, your favorite sheets, your friendships, whatever you have because he wants you to fail. He knows that the majority will simply give up and quit because it's hard.

This stain removal process is time consuming. In today's world if it doesn't come with a two-day Amazon Prime shipping schedule, we don't want it. Love is undervalued and isn't fought for anymore, its replaced. People don't know how to properly love anymore, and marriage is discarded like a piece of paper that doesn't mean anything. Speaking of that piece of paper, I have heard several people say, "*Everything was going smooth until we signed that paper,*" or "*Life was good until*

53

we got married." That's because that piece of paper isn't just a record for the state, it's proof of unity between husband and wife in the presence of the Lord. Marriage isn't a joke! That's why it's important to really love the person you are being united with. It's not going to be an easy ride.

Marriages not centered in God are satan's playground, and he plays hard on the equipment. There's a range of emotions he can swing on, he will make your thoughts a merry-go-round, and he will slide in to make your heart like sandcastles of doubt.

Satan will attack your self-image and your spouse's. We're drawn to looks and trends. Bless our hearts, if it doesn't have a set of abs and wear name brand clothes, we don't want it. What has this world come to? Let me let you in on a little secret.

Looks fade and so do abs. Yes, I said it. Shun me if you like. Neither will get you into heaven, friends, but a good foundation in the Lord will.

Replacing what you have with someone new is not the solution. There will still be issues and troubles, and you will have to deal with them. You can't replace something (or someone) every time your feelings get hurt or offended or things don't go your way. But you can ask God to give you insight on how to handle those issues in your relationship.

Our problem today is that we don't strip ourselves down and take the proper steps in the washing process. We don't take responsibility when the finger of guilt or responsibility is pointed at us. We only focus on trials when we believe we aren't the ones to blame. Then we allow that

55

stain to affect every fiber in our marriage. But if you stop this stain in its tracks, and refuse to let it sit and worsen, you stand a better chance of seeing transformative results.

What stain remover will you use? Those generic removers for my sheets are half price and I'm not hating on great value. That is my jam, anything to save a little money. But when we are dealing with eternal stains, I don't want something that's watered down. I don't want something that might work or perhaps will only lighten the stain a shade or two. I want the whole thing dissolved and gone. Discounted things may be the cheaper route for now, but it will cost you later. Don't mask these things with a cheap spray of, *oh, I'll do me, and you do you*. Get with the One who can strip this down and remove that stain.

We must *shout it out* to the Man upstairs and let Him sink His knowledge, wisdom, peace, and love into our hearts. The Lord is the "Shout" to all my stains, and I will gladly pay the extra price and take the necessary steps to remove all the built-up issues that I have let overtake my heart. God wants to work through every fiber in us. He wants to apply this product and watch us work through these things that we let hinder our marriage.

Depending on how long we have let these stains sit, it could take some scrubbing and reapplying of the Lord's grace and love. These seasons of life are hard, but they are only for a moment. We come out so much stronger in our faith and relationship with God if we just trust and obey Him. He will see you through this tough season.

Marriage is a set of *comfy* sheets but sometimes things we or our spouses do cause some hard-core stains that make our relationship not so comfy. Our problem is we don't strip ourselves right then and start the stain removal process. We are often so filled up with pride or self-pity that we only want to focus on what caused the issue or who is to blame. Then we let this negativity affect every fiber in us. If we can learn to stop this sin-filled ploy of the devil and refuse to harbor it in our hearts, then we have a better chance to see quick removal results.

You can swab it with that cheap generic version, or you can spray God's "Shout" on it and take effective steps that wash away the hurts and resentments, clear out unforgiveness and untrustworthiness, and blot up confusing stains *from your marriage. Isaiah 1:18-20 reads, "Come now, let us settle the matter," says the Lord. "Though your sins are like scarlet, they shall be as white as snow; though they are red as crimson, they shall be like wool. If you are willing and obedient, you will eat the good things of the land; but if you resist and rebel, you will be devoured by the sword." For the mouth of the Lord has spoken.*

Nothing compares to pulling freshly washed, stain-free sheets out of the dryer and wrapping yourself in them. And there is nothing as wonderful as a marriage that has been believed in and fought for and washed clean.

Reflection time...

What force is driving your mindset?

_____

_____

Have you been transparent with the Lord? _____

If not, do so. Lay it all out in front of Him.

What has God revealed to you that needs to change?

_____

_____

_____

Are you willing to take the necessary steps to

remove the stains causing division and animosity?

_____

Let God guide you through the process. Pray and

keep God as your driving force.

CHAPTER 5

LOVE

If we don't have love, we are nothing. In 1 Corinthians 13, Paul writes about how nothing we do will ever be worth anything if we don't have love. Love should be what drives you in everything you do. We are loved beyond measure by a God who sees our every move good or bad and He hears every thought that is in our mind that's never spoken.

For us to say we can't love anyone due to what they have done or said to us is not acceptable in God's eyes. Love covers a multitude of sins. Love is the most selfless act if it is done with the right intentions. There are four types of love and I will share a definition of each and how we have experienced that love.

EROS

One Greek word for *love*, describing erotic love like sexual or passionate love. The kind of love everyone seems concerned about. Our world is driven by sex and sexual appearances, which is what most people think love is all about. We are horribly mistaken.

Erotic love is a small portion of love. We take that part and blow it out of proportion when allowing sexual love before marriage. Unfortunately, it is nothing new, but normal for most people. For decades, even centuries, virginity has not been celebrated as sacred.

STORGE

Pronounced *stor-ghay,* is the second Greek word for *love*, refers to family love between a parent and a child or family members in general. Nothing compares to holding your child for the first time. It's a Divine experience, a softening love. The instantaneous love parents feel for their little baby when they meet for the first time is truly unspeakable.

Being surrounded by the ones who mean the most to us is another amazing feeling. So is loving on the ones who have loved us from day one and made efforts to create special memories to last for when they are no longer with us. This love is also one that the world is trying to distort and remove us from. Families are no longer together but segregated. And often, when the parent or grandparent who holds the family together is gone, families fall apart and move away from the true meaning of gathering and loving each other.

PHILIA

The third Greek word for love, which speaks of brotherly friendship and affection. Considered to be the highest love a man without God's help can feel and express.

We need these types of people around us, the ones who express *philia* love. They are good company. They typically are the few people we can count on for godly counsel in rough seasons. We rely on those who lift us up and have our backs but who aren't afraid to give corrective criticism to help us grow yet never harm us. We value those who hold us accountable for making right choices and point us in the direction of God. Marriage often starts as a form of friendship, which is an important form of love for it can grow in many directions.

AGAPE

The fourth Greek word for love. Although it is last on this list it is most important of all. The unconditional love that never changes under any circumstance or situation. It's a self-giving love that

65

gives without expecting anything in return. A love so great it can be given to those who are hard to love, who are unlovable or unappealing. It loves even when it's rejected. The person who extends agape love does so because he/she wants to.

The Bible says there is no profit for those who don't love. Self-sacrificial love is one of the most important ingredients in the stain removal process. Paul, in 1 Corinthians 13:4, gives a description of love. He isn't writing about how love is a feeling but how it's an action. He writes how love can be seen in our actions.

True love is always demonstrated in actions not in words. Paul lists the characteristics of love, and while his definitions may not be popular in our present culture, these are the very attributes needed in today's marriages and relationships. Let's take a look at them.

LOVE IS LONG SUFFERING

It suffers patiently. If God's love is in us, we will show long suffering to those who annoy us and hurt us. God has a long-suffering attitude toward us. I'm sure he probably shakes His head at us daily. He waits patiently for us to get our acts together and come back to Him. What an amazing God we serve!

LOVE IS KIND

When we understand God's love and show it to others, it will be seen in simple acts of kindness. Love should drive every move we make. We must deny ourselves and let the Word of God shape our thinking. Paul also talks about eight things love is not.

LOVE DOESN'T ENVY OR BOAST

Envy is when a feeling of discontent or resentful longing is aroused by someone else's possessions, qualities, or luck. It's a desire to have something that belongs to someone else. Envy is one of the least productive and most damaging of all sins. It accomplishes nothing but hurt. Love keeps a distance from envy and doesn't resent when someone else gets promoted or blessed. We are all guilty of envy whether we admit it or not. But when we know how love truly works, we begin to see the envy sins and move away from them.

When love shines the light on the dark then we can begin to recognize these things and work to

68

fix them. A heart that doesn't envy is content and wants to see others excel before themselves. Envy may seem like a small sin to us, but in the Bible it's not. Envy murdered Abel (Gen 4:3-8). Envy enslaved Joseph (Gen 37:11, 28. Envy put Jesus on the cross. "*For he knew that they had handed him over because of envy*" (Matthew 27:18). Envy is not small. It strips life from us, plants evil seeds, and destroys our relationships.

LOVE DOESN'T PARADE ITSELF

It doesn't insist on its own way. Love in action can work anonymously. Love doesn't need to be in the spotlight or have everyone's attention to do a good job. Love gives because it wants to and enjoys giving. It doesn't want praise. We should love regardless of what we are getting in return.

69

God loves us and yet we hardly give it back in return. Let's get real here. We are so blinded most of the time that we forget there is a loving God waiting patiently for us to be redeemed. Sometimes the people who seem to work the hardest at love are those the furthest from it. They do a lot of things that may be perceived as loving, yet they do it in a manner that's parading itself. This isn't love, it is pride looking for glory by the appearance of love.

LOVE IS NOT PUFFED UP

It's not arrogant, self-centered, or self-focused. Puffed up says, "look at me," and it speaks of someone who has a "big head" about things. Love doesn't focus on itself; it focuses on others. Parading and puffed up are similarly rooted in the pride seed of the enemy.

70

LOVE DOES NOT BEHAVE RUDELY

Where love resides, there will be kindness and good manner. This is not in a way of "look how cultured I am," but in a way that people don't behave rudely. Love is not offensively impolite, abrupt, nasty, harsh, or unpleasant. Love doesn't seek its own. Love doesn't just look out for itself. It doesn't look out for our own interest but having other people's best interest in mind.

This is being like Jesus in the most basic way. Jesus is in the people business, my friends. He was so others-centered that he died a horrible death to save people like me and you. We are called to have that same love. He has set the perfect example. It's up to us to be in this world and to learn what Jesus has done for us and appreciate it by striving to model Him in our lives.

We are planting seeds in our lives, our children's lives, and our spouse's life. Our actions reflect what we believe, and hopefully these actions demonstrate Jesus in us.

LOVE IS NOT PROVOKED

Provocation is when something or someone stimulates or gives rise to a reaction or emotion that's strong or unwelcome. It's a deliberate feeling of being annoyed or angry. We all find it easy to be provoked or to become irritated with those who are just plain annoying. But this is not love and it's a sin to give in to it. Moses was kept from the promised land because he became provoked by the people of Israel (Num.20:2-11). In my house, avoiding being provoked to annoyance is a daily battle and I fail 99.9% of the time. I'm thankful for a God that pours out so much grace over me.

Striving to be like Jesus is a goal we must all have and try to meet on the daily. None of us is perfect and we all fail, but as long as we are all pointed to Jesus His grace is sufficient, and we will all get there. God knows this. That's why He gave His son to die on that cross for us.

LOVE IS NOT EVIL

Love does not store up memories of any wrong it has received. Yes, that's right. Your little lock box of come backs and stored up anger has got to go. Bummer, I know. I too had to unload mine and it wasn't an easy task to do. But once you do life gets so much better. You feel lighter and more at peace. Although I thought that old stuff was useful, it really wasn't. I could only use it to hurt the one I loved the most. I was bottling up what used to hurt me just so I could turn around and do the same thing to my husband. Silly, if you really think about it.

In those times there was no example of love being set. We were just destroying each other spewing venom satan had planted in our hearts. You can't let the bad be stored up anymore. You have to forgive and move on. It doesn't matter how bad the hurt is, love conquers all.

Look at Jesus' life. He's the perfect example. Beat, battered, and bruised, yet He still loved till the end the ones who came against Him. Love will put away the hurt of the past instead of clinging to it. Real love never supposes that a good action may have a bad motive. The famous words in my house whenever someone does something sweet is "Okay, so what did you do wrong?" A prime example of assuming something was done with a bad motive. It strips the enjoyment from the one who was honestly trying to do something good.

LOVE DOESN'T REJOICE AT INIQUITY

It is willing to want the best for others and refuses to color things against anyone. Iniquity, for those who don't know, is immoral or grossly unfair, wicked, sinful behavior. We shouldn't rejoice in doing wrong but rejoice in the truth. Love can always stand with truth because it is pure and good like truth. Therefore running a grocery buggy into the side of someone's car at the store because they stole your parking spot is not love. It's wicked, sinful behavior. NO, I didn't do this, but I've watched it be done and that's why I park way at the back of the parking lot. No one wants a spot out there. Being spiteful and repaying evil for evil is exhausting.

I have found that when I get upset or mad, then I try to do something nice for the person that upset me. For instance, if my husband has tweaked my nerves and we have pulled the throwing-in-the-towel card like we talked about earlier in the book, I will find something to do for him. Doing something simple, like folding his clothes and putting them away, gives me a moment to reflect, and it takes that bitterness away. Serving him helps me to not be spiteful or retaliate negatively. I've learned that if I stay quiet while things are heated I have less to apologize for when all is said and done.

When you pause you can truly see your anger for what it is and what has caused it. I'm not saying pull out the silent treatment card, I'm just saying if you don't have anything nice to say don't say anything at all. Misunderstandings often occur as a result of hurt feelings, hateful words spoken or simple miscommunication. There is power in the pause.

In these verses Paul tells us a lot about what love *is* not, but he finishes strong with four more things that love *is*. Love is *strong, believing, hopeful, and enduring*. Spurgeon, who was an English Baptist preacher, calls these four virtues Love's Four Sweet Companions. Love *bears all things, believes all things, hopes all things, endures all things*. Paul uses the words "all things" and it means love covers *everything*.

LOVE BEARS ALL THINGS

We can all bear some things, we can all believe some things, we can all hope some things, and we can all endure some things. But God calls us to go deeper in our love for Him and for others. We must be prepared to love, no matter what.

Just like you and me, this world is imperfect. Unfortunately, we don't always get the best side of things presented to us. We must be ready and rooted in love to be able to handle "all things." Love doesn't ask to have an easy life. Love denies itself and sacrifices itself so it may win victories for God and not a cheap tinseled crown here on earth. When we study out "love bears all things" it means to carry the weight of something or to support or endure an ordeal or difficulty. But the word "bears" can also be translated as *cover*.

However you choose to word it, Paul brings up an important truth in 1 Peter 4:8: "*Above all things have fervent love for one another, for love will cover a multitude of sins.*" Love covers no matter which word you use to describe it. Love doesn't proclaim the errors of good men. Announcing someone's mess-up publicly isn't something done in love. We have all been guilty of this, anything to get the spotlight on someone else when things get heated. It's a common defense in this human culture, pointing out everyone else's flaws or mistakes so people don't see our own. But this act isn't fueled by love.

As sinful humans we are apt to spread bad news more than good news. Our sinful nature cannot wait to get that little piece of dirt on someone just so we can air it to our neighbor. We are constantly spreading seeds of the enemy when we do this. But our every action must be motivated by love. Spurgeon spoke this powerful line: "Love stands in the presence of a fault, with a finger on her lips."

I urge you to release the gift of gab! It's a harmful and sinful tool we all carry in our pockets. Instead, let's look at love as if it's an oyster. A piece of sand enters in an oyster's shell as a hurtful particle. When the oyster cannot eject this irritant, it covers it with a substance that is extracted out of its own life, which in turn changes this abrasive speck in to a pearl. We can do this in our own lives. By following Jesus' example we can take the hurtful, evil particles that enter our lives and cover them with love instead. We cover anger, resentment, or repaying evil for evil and turn it into something beautiful that will last far longer than our words.

LOVE BELIEVES ALL THINGS

We must choose to believe the best in others. We live in a perishing world and it's hard to believe anything we hear these days. But believing that there is going to be good that comes from all the evil around us is what being rooted in the love of God is all about. Some people habitually only believe the bad and never focus on the good. They are an example of children who don't know how to love. Wouldn't be nice if everyone only chattered of the good in one another and spoke only of the good deeds that are done among us? For once we could truly be bearers of good news.

LOVE HOPES ALL THINGS

Love has confidence in the future. When we suffer a hurt love doesn't say, "It will be this way forever" but rather love hopes for the best. Our hope is in God. Many times, we let self-pity strip our hope away from us. We let the enemy take over our minds and emotions. Before you know it the small argument you had about loading the dishwasher has turned into destruction in your own mind. You have divorced your spouse five times in your head over a spoon being put in the wrong slot! Your OCD is a preference and not everyone will do things the same way as you. You think I'm crazy, but you know what I'm talking about. We can take a small behavior and distort it into a huge issue if we don't have God at the center of our thoughts.

Don't think that you are imagining all these thoughts on your own. Satan will sneak in and create scenarios in your head about things that happened years ago, and you will immediately get mad all over again and be fighting about something that has already been put to rest. We must guard against the enemy's attack and hope for the best in all things. Regardless!

LOVE ENDURES ALL THINGS

To endure something is to stand firm under suffering or misfortune without yielding. Although this is difficult we must do it. Thinking about love and all that love does, enduring is probably the hardest. We live in a world where giving up has become the new normal. A world where, if it's hard, then you don't do it. Instead you find a shortcut to bypass the difficulty of the issue. We want fast solutions. If God's answer isn't on an Amazon shipping schedule, then we don't want it. We have conformed to a world that is molding us against what God has taught us to do. God knows there thing that are hard to understand and go through. Proverbs 3:5-6 tells us: "*Trust in the Lord with all your heart and lean not on your own understanding, in all your ways acknowledge him and he shall make your paths straight.*" Notice that He didn't say if you live a life close to Him that there wouldn't be difficulties to endure.

When living a life close to the Lord you are not only fighting against the world we live in today but a darker world in the spiritual realm. Everything about living a Christian life goes against today's normal. So that puts us in the "different" category and that "difference" really ruffles satan's feathers. We will look different when we stand out among the crowds and endure what has been thrown at us with the help of the Lord. There is a power that surrounds us and it's the power of Jesus.

All through the Bible we read about the troubles, trials, failures, sickness, plagues, famines, and deaths people had to endure. But we shouldn't focus on the negative of these harsh things when reading. We focus on the task at hand and we see that God brings good out of everything. For example, let's look at Job in the Bible. Job was a prosperous man of outstanding piety. The Bible says in Job 1 that he was blameless and upright, and he was one who feared the Lord and turned away from evil.

Let me make a little side note here. To fear the Lord doesn't mean to yield to Him out of being scared; it means to be in complete awe of him. It is a deep love and respect for the Lord putting Him above anything else. If you are living a life unpleasing to Him then yes, you should be scared because it's told to us what is to come if we don't live a life that's pleasing to Him.

Now back to Job. He was a man of plenty; he had the land, the animals, servants, and it's said that he was the greatest of all the people in the east. In all that Job was and had attained, God still had him endure some really hard times. God allowed satan to test him. He knew Job's faith, love, and respect was strong when He allowed everything that Job had to be given over to satan. The only thing the enemy couldn't have was Job's life. God said his life had to be spared.

So, satan went to work on the Lord's faithful servant. He took his property, his children, his livestock, and his servants. As soon as Job would get the news of one tragedy, another one would strike. In life we have these moments where everything just crashes down around us. It's one thing after another and we often blame God instead of having faith and trusting him. We let the pressure of the situation affect how we handle it. Many of us cradle under pressure and fall into failure mode.

In all that was happening to Job we read that he fell to his knees and worshipped the Lord. Let me say that again. In all that had happened he WORSHIPPED the Lord. I just needed to make sure we caught that part.

Job 1:20-22: *"Then Job arose and tore his robe and shaved his head and fell to the ground and worshipped." And he said, "Naked I came from my mother's womb, and naked shall I return. The Lord gave, and the Lord has taken away; blessed be the name of the Lord."* In all this, Job did not sin or charge God with wrong.

Whew... that's powerful! After all that had been taken from him, Job never once blamed God. He worshipped him instead. Satan didn't succeed with all the destruction he had caused upon Job because Job returned to God. The Lord again asked satan to consider his faithful servant Job and he replied, *"Skin for skin, all that man has he will give for his life. But stretch out your hand and touch his bone and his flesh, and he will curse you to your face."* Again the Lord handed over Job but said to spare his life.

Satan struck him with loathsome sores from the top of his head to the soles of his feet. Job's wife even tried to get him to let go of his integrity and curse the Lord. Still he did not. His friends came and didn't even recognize him, for his suffering was so great, and they too tried to turn Job away from the Lord. But they didn't succeed. Job never cursed God or blamed Him but expressed great grief about the day of his birth.

I tell you this story of Job, not to focus on all the trials and struggles, but to focus on his relationship with God. He had such a deeply rooted relationship with God that nothing that was thrown at him caused him to waver in his view of the Lord. In return for his great faith and active endurance during these dark times of loss and sickness God blessed him with double what he had before. His land and livestock and children and money were all given back in abundance. God was faithful to Job as He always is to us.

Just because we are close to the Lord doesn't mean troubles won't find us. I'm not saying that we are going to endure what Job did but we can learn from Job and his struggles. Today sickness paralyzes us, we lose loved ones, lose our jobs and possessions, but we can never lose our faith and relationship with the Lord when we are deeply rooted in His Word and ways. Satan lurks to and fro here on earth and he is always after us. Never forget that he is the lord of this world and all that's in it which is why things are the way they are now.

We can't take anything with us when we die and all our possessions will be dispersed, fought over, and thrown away once we leave this earth. I would rather leave a strong example of my relationship with the Lord and plant seeds of His goodness and righteousness in those I will leave behind. That's all that will truly matter in the end anyway. How faithful we are to God and His will and how we used our lives to minister to others is a legacy worth aiming for. So much of this world isn't for God and His goodness. This world pursues money, fame, lust, hate and everything opposite what God wants for us. We must remember why it is so important to have close relationship with our Creator.

Reflection time...

In your own words what is love?

_____

_____

_____

_____

_____

_____

Does your definition line up with 1 Corinthians

13:4—8? _____

If not tell how they are different?

_____

_____

_____

_____

_____

CHAPTER 6

Time Well Spent

Often, we shy away from what God has for us

because we don't understand His plan. We are

creatures of habit. The Bible is God's instruction

manual. It teaches us how to properly take on life

and all that it will throw at us. If we follow

instructions, then we will be molded into what God

has intended us to be. A lot of us don't understand

the Bible because it appears so intimidating, or we lack interest because of how complicated it seems.

But that's not the case. In both of those views it's because we are leaning on our own understanding. God doesn't call us to know it all. He just wants us to dig in and let Him teach us as we grow in Him. Spending time in His Word and creating that relationship with Him is what helps us understand His ways, His words, His thoughts, and His plan. God's divine plan for you and your marriage comes through a relationship with Him. It is not from sitting in a church pew or standing behind a pulpit or attending every seminar there is that involves the topic of Jesus. Don't get me wrong, those things are great but He will meet you right where you are to do kingdom work in you, your spouse, your home, and your workplace. You just need to allow Him to.

Your time will never be wasted when it's spent with Jesus. Let me give a little example here. Say you go to Target or Walmart or wherever and you purchase something that requires assembly. That product is going to come with a set of instructions. When you follow them, you're taking the time to read and understand what each step is instructing. By the last step you have created that pile of pieces into what it was intended to be. Not only is your product finished, but you have gained the knowledge of the instructions and how each piece has an important job.

This is the same with God's instructions. Wisdom gained can be used to help make someone else's assembly easier. Many times, we think we don't need instruction and we take matters into our own hands and make it more difficult than what it is supposed to be. We gain nothing but frustration and most of the time failure. God isn't the author of failure or confusion. He wants a deep relationship with you and me.

As I have stated many times throughout this book, He wants us to communicate with Him and believe and trust in Him. He wants us to dig into His Word and fully understand what it has for us. Just like the instruction manual, if we follow Jesus' instruction and gain His knowledge and wisdom from the living Word of the Bible, then we can apply it to our marriage and every other aspect of our lives and share as God has instructed us to do.

We all have testimonies that can help others, give inspiration to the ones struggling, and shed light on Jesus and His good works and how He saves. Each piece in the pile of our life parts has an important job. Not every piece is big and flashy. The majority of the time some of the smallest parts are the most important and valuable.

God doesn't call us to flash Him around. He calls us to apply His instruction to our lives and show others what we believe by our actions.

You're going to be a lot of things to many different people but most important is what you are to God. Time is never wasted when we are spending time with the Lord. Get into His word, research it, ponder it, memorize it, and follow each step God places in front of you. The finished product will be better than what you could possibly imagine. Apply His wisdom and knowledge and grace and forgiveness into your marriage and every relationship you are a part of and watch how things start to shift.

Those who aren't meant to be in your life will leave. Your perspective on life will change. And your heart will begin to mold into what the Lord intended it to be. We are all a box of pieces waiting to be put together but it's up to us on which way we choose to be assembled. We can be thrown together by our own free will with no instruction or guidance or we can let God guide each step and become the masterpiece He has created us to be. We are all a work in progress. Especially the husbands, right? Hehe. Just kidding.

CHAPTER 7

All-In-All

I want to leave you with some words of wisdom and some personal insight. Give grace. Grace literally means favor. We all mess up and do dumb things. You're not perfect and neither is your spouse. Life is short and we aren't promised tomorrow. Love your spouse and give him the best of you. Not because you think he does or doesn't deserve it, but because that's what God asks us to do. That's what you expect from him as well.

You can't expect the best out of someone else if you're giving nothing but the cold shoulder from your side. The Lord asks us to do good in everything we do. He tells us to not get diverted by things we can't control. He says to trust in Him and love like Jesus. We must choose to let go of our selfish ways and ambitions. Let go of our resentments, angers, unforgiveness, and hate. It's not worth holding on to.

Free yourself from the enemy's snares. Go against what's popular in this world and fight for your marriage. Stand out for your acts of kindness and love. Block all that causes disruptions and refuse to be caught up in things you cannot control. Love without expecting anything in return. Go the extra mile to help or make someone smile. Take the time to mend brokenness in your homes. Remove the stains and work through your problems.

Love like you want to be loved. This doesn't make you weak. Nothing in this life is perfect so get this out of your head. Your spouses are people too and they struggle just like you. They are going to do things that hurt you, disappoint you and annoy you, that's just life. It is not what they do that is important, but rather how you choose to let it affect you and how you handle it. Don't be influenced by what this world would have you to do. Be influenced by the One who wants the best for you. If you make a mess, clean it up. Do not be too proud to say I'm sorry.

You get one chance at life so make it count. Live, laugh, and love like there is no tomorrow. I can promise you this: when you leave this world your material things here on earth aren't going to mean a thing. But the relationship you made with the Lord will. Let Him guide you through this life and bless you with the little glimpses of heaven that are available here on earth. Let Him use you as a light tower so that His goodness can shine through you.

Leave a strong love example behind just like Jesus did for us. Build up your homes and guide them by God's instruction. Love those who are hard to love, for they need it the most. Being patient isn't a strong suit for me and I don't dare pray for God to help me with it. We all know the Lord has jokes sometimes. When you pray for help, He helps, just not how you might expect. If you don't believe me, pray for patience. You will gain it, but it might be a long process. I like to use a little reverse psychology for myself. Instead of praying for patience, I pray for active endurance and grace. Makes me feel better. I'm sure God just laughs and is like, "Okay, I see you!"

Have active endurance in your tough seasons and know that God is faithful and good will come out of it. Pray friends, pray. Communicate with God about everything, big or small. He will transform you in ways you have never imagined. Pray for one another. Pray for your spouse, your children, your friends, your family, your home, your jobs. Pray for everything. Don't forget to pray for me while you're at it.

We are at war. Let's rise and fight for the things that we are struggling with. Go against what's popular and mend those broken relationships. Love those who have wronged you. Wash the feet of those who have betrayed you, not because you're weak but because that's the key to refusing to be held prisoner by unforgiveness. You are releasing any power the devil has on you by not letting those things take root in your heart. Wash it with the blood of Jesus and move forward stain-free.

Take responsibility for your actions. When you're wrong, say your wrong. When you need to apologize, do so. Society has led us to believe this makes us weak or at the bottom of others. No, friends, it makes you strong. It makes you worthy. It makes you like Jesus. This world wants you to judge those who aren't in your circle. Stop judging. You don't know what battles people are fighting. You don't know what the devil has placed in front of them. Too often, judging others is what gives Christians a bad name. We are no better than anyone else. We sin with the rest of the world.

As a matter of fact, our sin is worse because we know better. We sling God's Word around like a sword cutting people with it, and forget that's not what it's used for. Don't be misinformed. The Word is used to fight battles with the evil that lurks with him, not to hurt each other. We need to be gentle, informative, and lead by example. We need to give grace. Grace is undeserved, unmerited, unearned favor. Practice grace wherever you go, especially in your homes, because that's the ultimate battlefield. Unity is honed there, and satan knows that. Give grace to your spouse and your children. If grace is practiced in the home, then it can be practiced in the world.

Finally, love yourself *too*. You're a child of God. He thought about you, and He created you just as you are. Don't forget where you were made. Let God's love reside in you, then shower it on others as He does for you. Love yourself enough to know that you are worthy of God's love and favor. You are important, you are seen, and He has heard your cry and seen your tears. He has been there in the challenging and good times, even though you don't always feel Him there. In a world full of darkness and uncertain times, cling to His garment, dig into His Word, and follow His instruction. Wash those stains that hold you captive in the devil's snare and love like there is no tomorrow, then *Be still and know that He is GOD* (Psalms 46:10).